Codebreakers Horizon

Codebreakers Horizon

NAVIGATING THE FUTURE OF PROGRAMMING TALENT

Anurag Anurag

Contents

1

Introduction

In the digital age, programmers are the architects of the future, crafting the code that powers our world. Yet, as critical as their skills are, the tech industry finds itself at a paradoxical crossroads: there's a burgeoning demand for programmers, but not just any programmers—the demand is for the truly adept, the problem-solvers, the creative thinkers, the ones who can turn complexity into simplicity. "Breaking the Code: Why Good Programmers Are Hard to Find" aims to dissect the multifaceted challenges that lead to this shortage.

We delve into the crux of the scarcity—where does the bottleneck lie? Is it in the education system that produces graduates less equipped for real-world programming challenges? Is it in the industry's unrealistic expectations or in its hiring practices that fail to capture a coder's true potential? Perhaps, it's within the nature of programming itself, a field that is as much about continuous learning and adaptability as it is about writing code.

This book dissects the ecosystem of programming talent—unveiling the disconnect between supply and demand, the traits that characterize top-tier programmers, and the systemic barriers that obstruct their discovery and development. It provides a roadmap for aspiring programmers, hiring managers, and tech leaders to bridge the gap and foster a future where the good programmers are not just found, but are nurtured and valued. As we break down these barriers, we offer insights into creating a more robust pipeline of talent ready to tackle the challenges of tomorrow's tech landscape.

The narrative of "Breaking the Code" reflects a truth all too familiar within tech circles: the hunt for proficient programmers is fraught with challenges and misconceptions. As the backbone of the ever-growing tech industry, programmers hold the keys to innovation. Yet, companies large and small voice a common dilemma—a difficulty in finding programmers who can excel beyond the baseline of coding to become visionaries of technology.

This perplexity invites a crucial question: Why is it so hard to find good programmers? Is it a deficiency within the realm of technical education, which might emphasize theory over practical, industry-relevant skills? Could it be the rapid pace of technological change, outstripping the ability of programmers to keep up? Or does the issue lie with the companies themselves, in their recruitment tactics and workplace cultures that may overlook or undervalue the full spectrum of a programmer's potential?

"Breaking the Code" seeks to illuminate these questions. It examines the pipeline that feeds the tech industry—from the classrooms where the first lines of code are written to the corporate strategies that attempt to harness talent. In exploring these stages, the book lays bare the disconnects and barriers that stymie the development and recognition of good programmers.

As we traverse from chapter to chapter, we will unpack the layers of complexity that characterize the programmer's ecosystem. We will look at how educational institutions can better align with the evolving needs of the tech industry and how companies can refine their search to not just fill positions, but to discover innovators. We'll explore the importance of fostering diverse and inclusive environments that can enrich the programming talent pool and consider the future skills that will be essential in the face of unceasing technological advancement.

This book is an invitation to rethink our approach to cultivating programming talent. It is a call to educators to inspire and to equip, a challenge to companies to seek out and to nurture, and an encouragement to programmers to aspire and to grow. Together, we can decode the mysteries behind finding good programmers and rewrite the future of tech talent development.

2

The Myth and Reality of the Programmer Shortage

In the heart of the digital revolution, a paradox exists: headlines scream of a programmer shortage, yet legions of coders struggle to find employment. This conundrum beckons us to scrutinize the data and narratives that shape our understanding of the technology job market. Is the shortage of programmers a statistical reality, or is it more nuanced, revealing instead a scarcity of candidates meeting the exacting standards of today's tech companies?

The crux of the matter lies in the interpretation of the data. Reports often suggest a dire need for more programmers, yet the nature of this need is seldom unpacked. Companies are not seeking just any programmer; they are on the hunt for individuals who are not only versed in modern programming languages but who also exhibit problem-solving prowess, adaptability, and the ability to continuously learn and grow in a fast-paced industry. The statistics reveal that while there is no shortage of people who can code, there is a gap when it comes to individuals who can meet these comprehensive, real-world demands.

Understanding the expectations of the industry is key to reconciling the supposed shortage with the reality of the job market. Today's tech companies are not just building websites or simple applications; they are developing complex systems that require a robust understanding of both software engineering principles and the business or application domain they are operating in. The qualifications necessary to perform at this level are substantial, and not all programming education paths are created equal in equipping their students with these skills.

The programmer shortage narrative often neglects to address the specific qualifications that are in short supply. These qualifications go beyond technical capabilities and encompass the softer, yet equally essential, skills such as effective communication, teamwork, and a strategic understanding of the business. It is here, in the chasm between the foundational knowledge taught in many computer science programs and the multidimensional expertise demanded by industry leaders, that the true shortage is most evident.

Understanding the roots of the programmer shortage requires a multi-dimensional analysis. While the tech industry continues to boom, with new startups appearing almost daily and established companies expanding their digital infrastructure, the demand for programmers far outstrips the available talent pool. Or does it? The statistics often cited in discussions about the shortage typically count the number of open positions against the number of computer science graduates. Yet, this fails to account for the complexity of what makes a programmer truly 'qualified' in the eyes of employers.

Further complicating the picture is the recruitment process. Traditional hiring practices may not be designed to detect the nuances of a programmer's expertise, especially when relying on keyword matching in resumes or focusing on narrow technical tests during interviews. As a result, the process can overlook talented individuals who may not match conventional criteria but possess the potential to excel with proper mentorship and opportunity.

The geographical distribution of programmers versus the location of tech jobs adds another layer of complexity. Although remote work has made strides in addressing geographic disparities, many companies still prefer local candidates or face challenges in managing distributed teams.

Amidst this landscape, recent graduates and self-taught programmers often find themselves in a Catch-22 situation. They are expected to have substantial portfolios and real-world experience, yet opportunities to gain such experience can be scarce without already having it. The industry's emphasis on practical experience over academic achievement or theoretical knowledge may exclude potentially talented programmers who have not had the opportunity to work on large-scale projects or in specific tech stacks.

There is the question of the global nature of the tech industry. While companies can tap into a worldwide talent pool, the complexities of international hiring, including legal, logistical, and cultural barriers, can impede the process. This global perspective is essential, as the demand for programmers is not uniformly distributed across the world, and neither is the supply.

The programmer shortage is not merely a matter of numbers; it is a multifaceted issue involving educational alignment, industry expectations, recruitment methodologies, and the global distribution of talent. Only by addressing each of these aspects can the tech industry begin to close the gap between the demand for skilled programmers and the available supply.

When assessing the reality of the programmer shortage, it's important to peel back the layers of what the term "qualified" encompasses. The definition is not static; it evolves as rapidly as the technology sector itself. In the past, proficiency in a few key programming languages might have sufficed. Now, the expectation includes a wide array of proficiencies, from cloud technologies to machine learning, and each subfield has its own set of complex frameworks and tools.

Moreover, the technical prowess that a programmer can demonstrate is often put to the test in a project environment that is collaborative and deadline-driven. The ability to integrate with an existing team and contribute meaningfully under pressure is a soft skill that is harder to quantify but no less critical. The discrepancy between the theoretical knowledge often imparted in academic settings and the practical know-how required on the job leads to a mismatch between graduating students and the roles awaiting them.

Another dimension to consider is the speed of technological obsolescence. Skills that were in demand just a few years ago might now be on the decline, replaced by new languages and paradigms. A programmer might be highly skilled in certain areas but find those skills less relevant to the market's current needs. This necessitates a continuous learning mindset and access to ongoing professional development, which not all programmers may have.

The burgeoning start-up culture and the lure of founding the next unicorn company also skew the programmer job market. These new companies often look for a very specific type of programmer: one who is not only a coder but also an innovator, willing to take risks and work long hours for the promise of equity and the excitement of rapid growth. This preference can make it harder for more traditional companies to find the talent they need, as they may offer less allure to the kind of entrepreneurial programmers who are drawn to start-up culture.

In the quest for programmers, there's also the issue of how the industry measures proficiency. Certification and formal qualifications are often disregarded in favor of portfolio work and evidence of practical experience. While this can help identify individuals with hands-on experience, it also creates barriers for those who have the theoretical knowledge but have not yet had the opportunity to apply it in a professional context.

The challenge of finding good programmers, therefore, is not just about identifying individuals with a current skill set. It's about finding individuals who can grow with the industry, adapt to new technologies, and contribute to a company's culture and success in meaningful ways. It requires a nuanced approach to hiring and education, one that accounts for the fluid nature of technical skills and the complex nature of software development as a collaborative endeavor.

In conclusion, the programmer shortage is a layered issue that cannot be captured by statistics alone. It is a dynamic interplay between evolving industry standards, educational practices, recruitment strategies, and the global distribution of talent. As the tech industry continues to advance at an unprecedented pace, the demand for programmers who are not only technically adept but also adaptable, collaborative, and innovative will only intensify.

This chapter has set the foundation for a thoughtful exploration into why good programmers are indeed hard to find. It invites us to look beyond the surface, to understand the nuances of the problem, and to acknowledge that addressing it will require concerted efforts across multiple domains. As we move forward, it becomes apparent that finding solutions to this shortage is as much about redefining what it means to be a 'good programmer' as it is about refining how we nurture and evaluate such talent. It is a challenge that calls for a comprehensive re-examination of the pipelines that bring new talent into the tech industry and the environments that allow them to thrive.

3

Educational Institutions vs. Industry Needs

The journey of a programmer traditionally begins in the hallowed halls of educational institutions where the fundamentals of computer science are imparted. However, as the digital landscape becomes increasingly complex, the alignment of academic curricula with the fast-paced, ever-evolving demands of the tech industry comes under scrutiny. This chapter delves into the effectiveness of these institutions in preparing students for programming careers, where the expectations of a classroom often differ from the realities of the workplace.

Higher education has long been the standard bearer for producing the next generation of programmers. Universities and colleges offer structured courses in theoretical concepts, algorithms, and data structures, which are undoubtedly the bedrock of programming knowledge. But, as technology advances, the gap between what is taught and what the industry requires seems to widen. The question arises: Are educational programs keeping pace with the rapid development of new programming languages, tools, and practices?

It's not uncommon to find fresh graduates well-versed in the academic aspects of programming but less prepared for the "real world" of software development. This preparation involves more than just writing code; it's about understanding how to work within a larger ecosystem. It includes version control, collaboration, writing unit tests, debugging, and the nuances of project management—areas that are often touched upon insufficiently in academic settings.

The discrepancy becomes evident when graduates enter the workforce. Employers frequently report the need for extensive on-the-job training to bring new hires up to speed with the practical, industry-ready expertise required for their roles. The industry's need for immediate contribution clashes with the time it takes for new programmers to acclimate to professional environments, suggesting a mismatch in expectations on both ends.

Furthermore, while academia tends to emphasize individual accomplishments, the tech industry operates largely on teamwork and collaboration. Projects often require programmers to integrate their work with that of others, navigate complex team dynamics, and communicate effectively with both technical and non-technical stakeholders—a shift from the solo endeavors of a university assignment.

Another dimension of this gap is the dynamic nature of industry needs, which can change within the time span of a four-year degree program. What students learn in their freshman year may be outdated by the time they graduate, rendering the skill set they have acquired less relevant. The onus is on educational institutions to incorporate industry trends into their curricula, an effort that requires continuous review and adaptation.

The tech industry is also marked by a culture of self-learning and constant evolution. Successful programmers often are those who engage in continuous learning, a trait that must be instilled during their education. Encouraging students to pursue side projects, contribute to open-source software, or participate in internships can bridge the gap between academic skills and practical expertise.

Understanding the symbiotic relationship between educational institutions and the tech industry is crucial. While the former provides the theoretical foundation, the latter molds that knowledge into the tangible skills needed to innovate and produce. Bridging the gap requires a concerted effort from both sides: for academia to adapt and update their teaching methodologies and content, and for the industry to actively engage in shaping educational programs that align with their evolving needs.

In this dynamic interplay between education and industry, there's a growing discourse on the model of education that would best serve the tech ecosystem. Some argue for a more hands-on, apprenticeship-style approach, where students can learn directly within the context of current industry projects. Others advocate for stronger industry partnerships with educational institutions to guide curricula that reflect the latest industry practices and expectations.

The traditional degree path is also being challenged by the proliferation of coding bootcamps and online courses, which promise to equip students with job-ready skills in a fraction of the time. These alternative educational avenues focus intensely on current programming languages and frameworks, and they often adapt quickly to industry changes due to their shorter curriculum cycles. However, while these programs excel in practical skills training, they may lack the comprehensive, foundational, theoretical education provided by a four-year degree, potentially leading to gaps in understanding that could hinder a programmer's ability to adapt to new technologies in the long term.

The evolution of technology has also led to the specialization of programming roles, which presents another challenge for educational institutions. A general computer science education may not delve deeply into the specialized knowledge required for fields such as data science, machine learning, or cybersecurity. The breadth of knowledge required to navigate these specializations can be vast and is often only touched upon at a surface level within the constraints of a general degree program.

Industry leaders and hiring managers often speak of a 'T-shaped' skill profile for ideal candidates, with deep knowledge and skills in one area (the vertical bar of the 'T') and the ability to collaborate across disciplines with a broad knowledge base (the horizontal bar). This model underscores the need for educational programs to balance depth and breadth in their offerings, to produce graduates who are both specialists in their field and versed enough in related areas to collaborate effectively.

As such, there's an imperative for educational institutions to not only impart hard skills but also to cultivate an environment that fosters innovation, encourages problem-solving, and prepares students for the interpersonal aspects of a programming career. This means integrating soft skills training, promoting teamwork through group projects, and exposing students to the industry as early and as often as possible.

Concurrently, the industry has a role to play in this educational evolution. Engaging with educational institutions through guest lectures, mentorship programs, internships, and curriculum development can help ensure that the skills being taught are those in demand. By creating a feedback loop, where industry needs are communicated back to educational institutions, a more responsive and agile educational model can emerge—

one that not only produces graduates with the right technical skills but also with a mindset attuned to the realities of a career in technology.

The intersection of educational institutions and industry needs is where the future of programming talent is shaped. Acknowledging and addressing the gap between academic skills and practical, industry-ready expertise is a critical step toward ensuring that this future is built on a solid foundation.

One aspect often overlooked in the dialogue between educational institutions and industry is the role of research and innovation within academia, which can be disconnected from the immediate practical applications desired by the tech industry. Universities are strongholds of research, pushing the boundaries of computer science, but this research can be highly theoretical, and its applications may not be immediately apparent or translatable to industry practices. Bridging this divide requires a dual approach where academic research informs industry innovation, and industry needs influence academic exploration.

In considering how to better prepare students for programming careers, there is also a need to address the variance in educational quality and opportunities across different regions and demographics. Access to quality education remains uneven, which can create disparities in the talent pipeline. As the tech industry increasingly recognizes the value of a diverse workforce, it becomes essential to ensure that educational opportunities in programming are inclusive and accessible to all.

Internships and co-op programs stand out as effective means for students to gain real-world experience while still in school. These programs provide a glimpse into the day-to-day work of programmers and offer a platform for applying theoretical knowledge in practical settings. Such experiences can be invaluable, bridging the gap between classroom learning and industry expectations by allowing students to develop a more nuanced understanding of their field and to build professional networks.

However, access to these opportunities is not universal, and often, the most beneficial experiences are highly competitive. Ensuring broader access to internships and cooperative education can help level the playing field, allowing a more diverse set of students to enter the job market with meaningful experience.

Moreover, there is an increasing need for continuous professional development within the programming profession. As the half-life of tech skills continues to shrink, the concept of education as a one-time, pre-career endeavor becomes outdated. Instead, there is a shift toward lifelong learning models where education is an ongoing process, and programmers are expected to continually update their skills. Educational institutions can support this by offering modular, flexible learning options that allow for skill updates without the need for extended time away from the workforce.

Finally, while the responsibility for bridging the education-industry gap is shared, the ultimate success of a programmer is often self-determined. In an industry that values self-starters and continuous learners, the ability to take initiative and pursue personal development is paramount. The role of education is thus not just to teach skills, but to instill a mindset of growth and a habit of lifelong learning. With these attributes, programmers can navigate their careers in an industry where change is the only constant, and adaptability is key.

4

∽

The Journey to Mastery: What Makes a Programmer Good?

Mastering programming is a complex and ongoing process, a voyage rather than a definitive endpoint. This evolution is about developing a rich tapestry of skills that weave together to create the fabric of a proficient technologist. The real essence of a capable programmer is found not just in their ability to churn out lines of code, but in a broader, more comprehensive skill set that understands the complex ecosystem of software development.

Such proficiency encompasses a broad knowledge base, from multiple programming languages to the application of various paradigms at the right time. Proficient programmers carry a depth of knowledge that runs deep—intimate with algorithms, data structures, and design patterns. Their code is more than functional; it's crafted to be maintainable, scalable, secure, and robust against a host of potential challenges.

The technical expertise of these individuals is a critical piece of the puzzle, but it's just one aspect of their capability. They have an acute sensitivity to user experience, preemptively navigating the needs and challenges of end-users. Their strategic foresight allows them to plan beyond the current scope of projects, looking ahead to future requirements and evolutions. As systemic thinkers, they are able to understand and influence the broader architecture of the systems they contribute to, ensuring their work aligns with overarching business goals.

Such individuals are quintessential team players, equipped with the communication skills necessary to translate complex technical issues into clear terms for collaboration. Their contributions enhance team dynamics, often serving as mentors and learning from peers with varied expertise. They excel in diverse, dynamic environments where collaboration is key.

The road to this level of proficiency is lined with a constant curiosity and an unwavering dedication to learning—a journey that doesn't wane with time or success. For these programmers, staying abreast of technological advancements is not a chore but a passion that is integral to their craft. This zeal drives them to explore new languages, embrace cutting-edge technologies, and refine their craft continuously.

This commitment often sees them actively participating in the broader tech community, contributing to open-source projects, attending conferences, and staying attuned to the latest research. They understand that programming is a communal activity, where growth is fueled by exchanging ideas and collaborating with a global network of peers.

The programming journey is interlaced with continuous knowledge accumulation, skill expansion, and a growing enthusiasm for the discipline. Every new competency gained, every problem resolved, and every project completed propels them toward greater challenges and achievements.

As technology becomes an omnipresent force in modern life, the significance of the programmer's work is magnified. They are the visionaries and creators behind the scenes, building the tools that empower, entertain, connect, and increasingly integrate into every facet of our existence. This substantial role demands a profound commitment to quality, ethical integrity, and a conscious approach to the potential impact of their work.

The defining qualities of proficient programmers are built on a solid foundation of technical skill, flexibility in methodology, ethical responsibility, cooperative spirit, and an enthusiasm for lifelong learning. Their development is a process of continuous growth, fueled by a passion not just for solving technical problems, but for making meaningful contributions to the world through technology.

These programmers are not just coding technicians but visionaries capable of foreseeing and even driving the changes that mold the future. They recognize patterns of technological evolution and position themselves to take advantage of the new opportunities that arise.

The programming journey embodies various forms of passion—it's seen in the meticulousness of their craft, the perseverance in debugging, the satisfaction in optimization, and the joy in knowledge sharing. This enthusiasm leads them to mentor and elevate their peers and the collective, transforming individual endeavors into a shared quest for excellence.

The broad pursuit of programming involves understanding not just the technical but also the human elements of development—the users, the team dynamics, the business context, and the societal repercussions.

The trajectory of a programmer's career is self-directed. They are the architects of their education, blending formal instruction with self-led learning, experimentation, and community engagement. They create personal environments conducive to growth, setting their benchmarks, and consistently striving to surpass them.

In a world where technology and change are synonymous, programmers are adaptable professionals who navigate this terrain with resilience and agility. Comfortable with ambiguity, they learn swiftly on-the-go—a necessity in an industry defined by quick innovation and ongoing transformation.

The qualities that characterize a proficient programmer converge at the nexus of expertise, curiosity, passion, and unceasing growth. Their development is not linear but cyclical, involving learning, application, reassessment, and innovation—a cycle that is both deeply personal and interconnected with the broader narrative of the tech community and society.

As programming intertwines with societal fabric, programmers take on a crucial role not only in crafting tools and platforms but also in guiding the direction of societal engagement with technology. They approach their responsibilities with societal stewardship in mind, contemplating the wider implications of their output.

In the grand scheme, the proficient programmer's path is not a solitary one; it is enriched by the culture of shared knowledge and collaborative innovation. They engage in community discourse, contribute to the collective codebase, and participate in forums where challenges are addressed collectively. These interactions not only propel their personal growth but also advance the field of programming as a whole.

The personal dimension of this journey is characterized by introspection and self-management. Proficient programmers develop personalized strategies for tackling complex problems and for assimilating new knowledge. This self-knowledge enables them to leverage their strengths effectively and to identify areas where further growth is needed, allowing for a tailored approach to their professional development.

Moreover, the proficient programmer's repertoire of skills increasingly includes insights from other disciplines, acknowledging the interconnectedness of programming with various aspects of life and business. They may draw on design to enhance usability, delve into psychology to better understand user interaction, or incorporate elements of project management to deliver solutions that are not just technically sound but also commercially viable.

Creativity and innovation are central to the programming ethos. Proficient programmers are not content with the status quo; they challenge existing paradigms and push beyond the known boundaries of technology. Their careers are punctuated with instances of bold thinking and inventive solutions, underscored by a willingness to embrace and learn from failures.

This journey, then, is not merely a professional endeavor but a personal commitment to an ongoing process of evolution, reflecting the fluid nature of technology itself. It's a dedication that goes beyond the individual, impacting the collective workspace, and extends to society at large. Proficient programmers understand that their contributions are part of a larger narrative that tells the story of human progress and our shared pursuit of pushing the boundaries of the possible.

Navigating the technological landscape with purpose and a commitment to lifelong learning, programmers become both the creators and custodians of the future. Holding a vision of technology's potential, they continuously refine their skills and insights with each step forward, perpetually on a path to mastery that is as intellectually demanding as it is rewarding.

This path to mastery in programming also requires a strong ethical framework. Developers recognize that their coding decisions and innovations have significant societal impacts. They undertake their work with a deep sense of responsibility, prioritizing the security, privacy, and ethical usage of their creations to ensure technology serves the greater good and does not cause harm.

This ethical awareness goes hand in hand with a commitment to inclusivity and accessibility. Developers strive to make sure the technologies they create are accessible to everyone, including those with disabilities. They promote diversity not only in their code but also within their teams and the broader tech community, fostering a range of perspectives that enhance innovation and lead to fairer, more inventive technological solutions.

In striving for excellence, these developers balance confidence with humility. While they trust in their abilities and knowledge, they remain open to learning and acknowledge their own limitations. This balance encourages a collaborative environment, conducive to the free exchange of ideas and the flourishing of innovation.

Furthermore, the journey to becoming a skilled developer is characterized by a proactive approach to problem-solving. Rather than merely reacting to issues as they arise, they anticipate potential challenges and strategize appropriate solutions ahead of time. This forward-thinking mindset not only bolsters the robustness of their projects but also ensures they are well-prepared to adapt to changes and surmount obstacles efficiently.

The essence of a skilled developer's path is the synthesis of expertise, ethics, and collaboration. It is a multifaceted development process that involves enhancing technical abilities, deepening interpersonal relationships, and continually adapting to the changing technological landscape.

Ultimately, the journey of a skilled developer is about much more than just mastering programming languages or technologies; it's about fostering a mindset geared towards growth, innovation, and responsible creation. It's about building a career that is not only successful but also meaningful and in harmony with broader societal values.

As technology increasingly permeates every facet of human life, the role of the developer becomes ever more pivotal. The future of programming isn't just about spearheading technological advancements but also about guiding how these advancements shape our world. With their profound insights and proactive attitudes, skilled developers are crucial in ensuring that this future is as promising and beneficial as possible.

Their continuous journey reflects a dedication not only to personal and professional development but also to making positive contributions to the community and the world at large. It is a path marked by relentless learning, ethical integrity, and a commitment to enhancing the human experience through technology. Thus, skilled developers stand at the vanguard of shaping the future, their endless quest to explore, create, and improve both the digital and the human landscapes.

In conclusion, the journey of mastering programming is not solely about acquiring technical skills or mastering the latest technologies; it is fundamentally about embracing a holistic approach that combines profound technical proficiency with ethical awareness, collaborative spirit, and a commitment to continuous improvement. Developers who excel in their field do so not just through their coding prowess but through their ability to foresee and navigate the complex interplay between technology and society.

This comprehensive approach ensures that their contributions are not only innovative and effective but also responsible and inclusive, reflecting a deep understanding of the broader implications of their work. By balancing their technical abilities with an ethical compass and a dedication to community and personal growth, they set a standard for what it means to be a truly skilled developer.

The path these developers walk is one of endless learning and adaptation, shaped by both the challenges they encounter and the achievements they celebrate. It is a journey that demands a dynamic blend of skills, a forward-thinking mindset, and an unwavering commitment to improving not just their own capabilities but the world around them.

As we wrap up this chapter, we recognize that the essence of becoming a skilled developer lies not just in what they know or can do but in how they apply their knowledge and skills to make a positive impact. It is a continuous pursuit of excellence, innovation, and ethical practice that defines their professional identity and their invaluable role in shaping the future of technology and society.

5

Hiring Conundrums: Identifying True Talent

The process of hiring in the tech industry is fraught with challenges, a complex puzzle that organizations must solve to secure the talent that will drive their success. Traditional hiring practices, often characterized by the familiar funnel of resume screening followed by technical interviews, have long been the standard. Yet, questions persist about their efficacy in truly identifying the best candidates.

Resume screening often serves as the first gatekeeper in the hiring process. It is a method aimed at filtering out applicants based on a set of predefined criteria, such as specific skills, experience levels, and educational backgrounds. However, this approach can be myopic, potentially excluding candidates with unconventional career paths or diverse experiences that don't translate well on paper. Moreover, the reliance on keyword matching can overlook those who may excel in less quantifiable attributes like problem-solving ability, creativity, and teamwork.

Following the resume review, candidates typically progress to technical interviews, which are designed to assess their coding skills and technical knowledge. While these interviews can offer insights into a candidate's technical capabilities, they can also be limited in scope, focusing too narrowly on specific problems or technologies. This can result in a failure to gauge a candidate's broader problem-solving approach or their ability to learn and adapt to new technologies—traits that are essential in the fast-paced tech industry.

Furthermore, technical interviews often underemphasize soft skills that are crucial for successful teamwork and project management. Communication, empathy, and the ability to collaborate effectively are frequently sidelined in favor of technical prowess, despite being key components of a successful programmer's skill set.

This traditional hiring funnel also tends to be an anxiety-inducing experience for candidates, which can further obscure true talent. High-pressure coding challenges and algorithmic puzzles may not accurately reflect a programmer's day-to-day work and can disadvantage otherwise qualified individuals who do not perform well in such settings.

In light of these shortcomings, there is a growing recognition of the need for alternative approaches to uncovering and recognizing programming talent. Innovative companies are rethinking their hiring strategies, exploring new methodologies that aim to reveal a candidate's true potential beyond the resume and technical interview paradigm.

One such approach involves more practical, project-based assessments. Candidates are given a small-scale project or task that closely mimics real-world responsibilities. This method provides insight into how a candidate approaches problem-solving, manages their time, and overcomes obstacles, offering a more accurate representation of their potential on-the-job performance.

Pair programming is another technique gaining traction, where a candidate collaborates with an existing team member on a problem during the interview process. This not only demonstrates the candidate's technical skills in a collaborative environment but also gives both parties a taste of what the working relationship would entail.

Some organizations are also placing greater emphasis on behavioral interviews that delve into a candidate's past experiences and approaches to various scenarios. These interviews can uncover invaluable information about a candidate's soft skills, work ethic, adaptability, and how they may fit into the company's culture.

Moreover, companies are considering candidates' contributions to open-source projects, hackathons, and other collaborative tech communities as a measure of their passion, collaborative spirit, and real-world coding experience. Such contributions can be indicative of a candidate's dedication to the craft of programming and their ability to work effectively with a team.

There's also a move towards more inclusive hiring practices that seek to diversify the tech workforce. This includes creating job descriptions that are inclusive, using software that mitigates unconscious bias, and ensuring that interview panels are diverse.

As the tech industry continues to evolve, so too must the methods for identifying and recruiting the people responsible for driving innovation forward. It's becoming increasingly clear that finding the right match for a programming role is a nuanced endeavor that requires looking beyond traditional metrics and methods. By adopting a more holistic and innovative approach to the hiring process, organizations can better position themselves to discover and attract the kind of talent that will not only fill a current need but will also contribute to the company's growth and evolution over time.

Expanding on the concept of holistic hiring, companies are increasingly looking to tap into the rich potential of candidates who may bring a wealth of transferrable skills from different industries or backgrounds. By valuing diversity of thought and experience, employers can foster a culture of innovation and resilience. This is particularly relevant in an industry where adapting to and integrating new perspectives can be the key to breakthroughs and staying ahead of the curve.

Embracing a candidate's potential for growth is another aspect of this evolved hiring process. Instead of focusing solely on current skills, more emphasis is placed on the ability and eagerness to learn, which is essential in an industry defined by constant change. Assessing a candidate's learning curve and their enthusiasm for self-improvement can be more indicative of long-term success than their existing knowledge base.

The role of data analytics in hiring is also becoming more prominent. By leveraging data, employers can make more informed decisions about which candidates are likely to succeed. This involves analyzing patterns and outcomes of past hiring decisions to refine the criteria and processes used to evaluate candidates.

Networking events, both virtual and in-person, are also proving to be fertile ground for identifying talent. Such environments allow for more natural interactions and can provide insights into how candidates engage with peers and potential employers. They also give candidates the opportunity to showcase their communication and interpersonal skills in a less formalized context than the traditional interview.

Furthermore, internal referral programs can be an effective way of discovering talent. Current employees can often identify individuals within their networks who not only have the technical skills but also the right fit for the company's culture and values. These referrals can come with built-in endorsements of the candidate's work ethic and collaborative abilities.

To complement these innovative approaches, some companies are revisiting the role of education and credentials in their hiring criteria. While a solid educational background can be indicative of a candidate's skills, there is a growing appreciation for self-taught individuals and those with non-traditional education paths. Their drive for self-improvement and ability to self-motivate can be particularly valuable in a field where learning on the job is a constant necessity.

In this new hiring landscape, the journey from candidate screening to final interview is less a series of hoops to jump through and more a cohesive process aimed at understanding the whole person. It's about creating opportunities for engagement that reveal not just how a candidate thinks, but how they learn, collaborate, and contribute to a collective mission.

The tech industry's approach to hiring is thus shifting from a transactional model to a relational one, recognizing that the process is not simply about filling a vacancy but about building a relationship. It's about inviting someone into a shared journey of growth, innovation, and collective achievement. In recognizing the complexity of this task, companies are devising more nuanced and comprehensive methods to identify the true artisans of the digital age.

In continuing to refine the hiring process, forward-thinking companies are also investing in long-term talent development, beginning with internships and apprenticeships that allow for the cultivation of promising individuals. This investment reflects a recognition that potential can be nurtured and that the right environment and mentorship can transform good candidates into great employees.

The value of ongoing dialogue with the educational sector is also being recognized. Establishing partnerships with universities and coding boot-camps can provide a direct line to emerging talent. These collaborations can help tailor educational programs to better match industry needs, ensuring that graduates are equipped with the skills and knowledge that are in high demand.

Another developing trend is the use of simulations and virtual environments to assess candidates' problem-solving abilities in real-time. Simulations can replicate the kind of challenges programmers will face on the job, providing a clear picture of how a candidate might perform in the role. This approach tests not only technical skills but also the ability to think critically and work under pressure.

Social media and online presence are increasingly important aspects of a candidate's profile. Employers are looking at how candidates present themselves online, their engagement with tech topics, and their broader interest in the field. A well-maintained GitHub repository or a thoughtful tech blog can speak volumes about a candidate's dedication and expertise.

In the quest for talent, companies are also reconsidering the value of soft skills. The ability to adapt to change, to work well within a team, and to lead with empathy are becoming as prized as technical abilities. Soft skills assessments are being integrated into the hiring process to ensure that new hires will enhance the team dynamic and company culture.

At the same time, there's an increasing emphasis on the candidate experience throughout the hiring process. A transparent, respectful, and communicative approach not only reflects well on the company but also helps engage potential hires. A positive hiring experience can have a lasting impact on a candidate's view of the company and increase the likelihood of accepting an offer if extended.

Moreover, as remote work becomes more prevalent, the ability to work effectively in a distributed team is becoming a key consideration. This has led to the inclusion of remote work simulations as part of the hiring process, where candidates demonstrate their ability to communicate and collaborate effectively in a virtual setting.

As the tech industry continues to evolve at a rapid pace, so too must the strategies for identifying and attracting the individuals who will drive its future. By embracing a more holistic and innovative approach to the hiring process, organizations can better position themselves to discover the talent that will not only meet the technical demands of today but will also contribute to the innovation and success of tomorrow.

On the complexities of hiring in the tech industry, it's evident that identifying true talent requires an approach that goes beyond the conventional. The traditional hiring funnel—rooted in resume screening and technical interviews—while not without merit, often fails to capture the multifaceted nature of programming expertise and potential.

As the tech landscape continues to advance, so does the understanding that the ideal candidate is often more than the sum of their technical skills. It's the blend of creativity, critical thinking, teamwork, and adaptability that often signals true talent. Therefore, alternative approaches to hiring are not just innovative but necessary. They encompass a broader vision of what it means to be a proficient developer, a team member, and a contributor to the field.

These alternative approaches advocate for a hiring process that's as dynamic and multifaceted as the candidates it seeks to attract. By incorporating practical assessments, project-based evaluations, and a focus on soft skills and cultural fit, companies can gain deeper insights into a candidate's true potential. In looking beyond the resume and considering the whole person—their passions, their learning trajectory, their collaborative spirit—organizations can make more informed decisions.

The evolving hiring strategies discussed are more than just methods for evaluating candidates; they reflect a larger shift in the industry towards greater diversity, inclusivity, and a recognition of different paths to programming proficiency. They are about building relationships and investing in talent that will grow alongside the company.

Ultimately, as this chapter concludes, it leaves us with a renewed perspective on the importance of thoughtful, comprehensive hiring practices. The tech industry's continued prosperity hinges not just on the skills developers bring today but on their potential to innovate, adapt, and contribute to an ever-changing technological frontier. The quest for talent, therefore, is also a quest for those who will not only navigate the future but shape it.

6

The Cultural Fit Puzzle

The tech industry, celebrated for its innovation and dynamism, has come to recognize that coding prowess alone does not a perfect candidate make. There's a growing awareness of a different set of criteria—often intangible and harder to measure—that is just as critical to an individual's success within a company: soft skills, teamwork, and adaptability. These elements collectively comprise what is often referred to as "cultural fit," the harmonious alignment of a candidate's values, behaviors, and beliefs with the core ethos of an organization.

Soft skills—such as effective communication, conflict resolution, and empathetic leadership—are crucial. They are the lubricant that keeps the gears of a team moving smoothly. In the intense collaborative environment of tech projects, the ability to articulate ideas clearly, listen to others, and give and receive feedback constructively can make the difference between a project's success or failure.

Teamwork, too, is indispensable. The best solutions in technology are seldom the product of isolated genius but rather the result of collective effort. A programmer who is adept at fostering a collaborative spirit, who can inspire and be inspired by their teammates, is a valuable asset. This collaborative prowess often extends beyond one's immediate team to include cross-departmental cooperation, making the ability to navigate and synthesize a diversity of perspectives and expertise especially important.

Adaptability is another pillar. In an industry characterized by rapid change, the ability to pivot and embrace new methods, tools, and technologies is vital. A candidate's track record of learning, unlearning, and relearning is a strong indicator of their potential for long-term success.

Cultural fit is where these attributes converge, and it's increasingly a focal point in the search for the best programming talent. Organizations are aware that an employee who aligns with their values and work style can not only excel in their individual role but also contribute positively to the work environment, boosting morale and promoting a productive and innovative workplace.

Identifying cultural fit, however, is less straightforward than assessing technical skills. It involves peering into the subtleties of a candidate's character and work philosophy, often through behavioral interviews, work simulations, and team interactions. It's a complex puzzle, seeking to determine how an individual will mesh with the existing company culture and whether they will thrive within it.

Some companies place such a high premium on cultural fit that they prioritize it over technical skills in their hiring decisions, subscribing to the belief that technical skills can be taught but cultural fit cannot. They invest in individuals who demonstrate a strong alignment with the company's core values and vision, betting on the long-term benefits of such alignment.

Yet, the emphasis on cultural fit comes with its own set of challenges. There is a fine line between a harmonious workplace and a homogenous one. A company must be careful to ensure that their definition of cultural fit does not exclude diversity of thought, background, and approach. After all, it's often the fresh perspectives that drive innovation.

In the quest to solve the cultural fit puzzle, organizations are refining their interview techniques to uncover these soft qualities. Behavioral questions aimed at revealing how a candidate has handled past situations are common. Employers are interested in stories that demonstrate conflict resolution, teamwork, adaptability to change, and growth from failures. These narratives give color to the candidate's interpersonal skills and problem-solving approach, offering a glimpse into how they might contribute to the company's culture.

Workplace simulations and group interviews also provide a platform for observing candidates in action, allowing employers to see firsthand how they interact with others. These scenarios can reveal nuances in behavior that aren't as apparent in one-on-one interviews, such as how candidates deal with stress, collaborate on tasks, or assume leadership roles when necessary.

Moreover, some companies are involving team members in the hiring process to assess the potential for chemistry between existing employees and candidates. This practice recognizes that every team has its unique rhythm and that a new hire should be able to move in step with the existing cadence. It's an approach that seeks to preserve team harmony and productivity.

It's also becoming more common for companies to articulate their culture and values clearly in job descriptions and recruitment materials. By communicating what the organization stands for and the type of work environment it fosters, potential applicants can self-select based on their alignment with these values. This transparency helps attract candidates who are more likely to fit well with the company culture.

As much as cultural fit is about harmony, it's also about balance. A successful team needs a range of personalities—leaders and listeners, visionaries and executors, challengers and collaborators. Therefore, the hiring process must be designed to recognize and appreciate this diversity. A well-rounded team, united by shared values but rich in diverse perspectives and approaches, is often the most robust.

On the flip side, too rigid a focus on cultural fit risks creating an echo chamber, stifling innovation and diversity. Thus, progressive companies strive to find the sweet spot where a strong cultural core coexists with diverse, dynamic individuals who can bring new ideas and approaches to the table. They seek candidates who not only align with the company's values but also expand its horizons.

The cultural fit puzzle is not just about fitting into the current culture but also about contributing to its evolution. It's about finding individuals who can grow with the company, shaping and being shaped by its culture over time. This dynamic interplay between the individual and the organization is what keeps a company's culture vibrant and relevant.

In this light, cultural fit becomes less about conformity and more about synergy—the creation of a dynamic environment where the whole becomes greater than the sum of its parts, powered by individuals who are both aligned and uniquely themselves. This chapter explores how identifying and nurturing this synergy can be key to building teams that will thrive and drive innovation in the tech industry.

This exploration of cultural fit also includes a critical examination of onboarding processes. After the hiring phase, onboarding is the next critical step where new hires are immersed into the company culture. Effective onboarding programs don't just introduce the nuts and bolts of daily operations but also encapsulate the spirit of the organization, helping new employees to understand not just what the company does, but why it does it, and how each role contributes to the larger mission.

Moreover, the approach to cultural fit is also evolving in terms of ongoing employee engagement and development. Companies are realizing that cultural fit isn't a static attribute assessed at hiring but a dynamic quality that needs to be fostered continuously. Regular check-ins, professional development opportunities, and team-building activities can ensure that employees remain in tune with the company culture and values as both evolve.

Feedback mechanisms are integral to this process, allowing both employees and management to express how they see the culture and their place within it. This ongoing dialogue ensures that the company remains a living ecosystem, responsive to the needs and growth of its people.

Additionally, there is a growing emphasis on cultural contribution over cultural fit. Instead of looking for candidates who 'fit' into the existing culture, there's a shift towards seeking those who will contribute to it positively. This distinction emphasizes the role of individuals in enriching and enhancing the company culture, bringing in new ideas and practices that could lead to its betterment.

The broader implications of this approach can't be understated. It shifts the perspective from maintaining the status quo to embracing change and growth. It ensures that a company's culture doesn't become stagnant but instead remains a competitive advantage, helping to attract and retain the best talent.

The cultural fit puzzle, therefore, is not simply about matching individuals to a predefined mold. It's about creating a culture that is both robust and flexible, capable of integrating new elements while maintaining its core identity. It's about recognizing the transformative power that each new hire holds, not just in their capacity to perform their job, but in their potential to influence the very fabric of the workplace.

As companies navigate the intricate dance of assembling teams that are cohesive yet diverse, stable yet adaptable, and aligned yet open to change, the true complexity of the cultural fit puzzle becomes evident. It's a challenge that requires a nuanced and thoughtful approach, one that appreciates the multifaceted nature of creating a productive and innovative workplace. This chapter underscores the critical role that understanding and managing cultural dynamics plays in the search for, and retention of, programming talent in the modern tech landscape.

In seeking a solution to the cultural fit puzzle, it becomes essential to consider the long-term trajectory of team development. Cultivating a team isn't just about selecting individuals who can work together today; it's about envisioning how they will grow and interact in the years to come. Leaders are tasked with not only recognizing present compatibility but also with fostering an environment that encourages evolution, learning, and the meshing of diverse talents over time.

Part of this foresight involves looking at potential rather than just present compatibility. A candidate who may not seem like a perfect cultural fit initially might possess the adaptability and growth mindset to blend into and eventually enhance the company culture. Hiring for potential invites a more dynamic understanding of cultural fit—one that is less about ticking current boxes and more about drawing lines to future growth.

Another dimension of the cultural fit puzzle is the alignment of personal and organizational goals. Employees who see their personal growth and aspirations reflected in the company's trajectory are likely to feel more engaged and motivated. This alignment fosters a sense of shared purpose and drives collective effort towards common goals.

Moreover, as companies scale and diversify, the challenge of maintaining a cohesive culture while also allowing for subcultures becomes significant. Subcultures within departments or teams can be powerful, as they reflect the specialized nature of different areas of work. Yet, they need to harmonize with the overarching company culture to ensure unity and a sense of belonging among all employees.

Companies also face the task of integrating remote and global team members into the company culture. In a world where teams are often spread across time zones and cultures, creating a unified yet flexible culture that accommodates this diversity is vital. It requires intentional communication strategies, shared experiences, and inclusive policies that bring remote team members into the fold of the company's day-to-day life.

As we delve deeper into the cultural fit puzzle, it becomes apparent that it's a complex interplay of many factors—individual personalities, team dynamics, organizational goals, and the broader societal context. Solving this puzzle isn't about finding people who fit the mold but about building a mosaic of talents and perspectives that, together, form a vibrant and effective whole.

It's a delicate balance, creating a culture that is both distinct and inclusive, stable and adaptable, united and diverse. Companies that succeed in this endeavor create not just a workforce but a community—one that can navigate the complexities of the tech industry with agility and cohesion. This community becomes the company's bedrock, driving innovation, excellence, and a shared sense of purpose.

Navigating the cultural fit puzzle is, therefore, an ongoing process of understanding, integrating, and harmonizing the varied human elements that make up a company. It's about crafting a culture that embraces diversity, fosters growth, and aligns individual aspirations with collective objectives. As organizations continue to puzzle out this complex task, those that do so with thoughtfulness and agility find themselves building not just teams but a resilient and dynamic culture capable of enduring the tests of a rapidly evolving industry.

Recognizing the nuances of cultural fit involves understanding that the work environment itself can be a catalyst for individual transformation. A company culture that encourages learning, development, and mutual respect can shape individuals, just as they contribute to the culture. The impact of this bidirectional influence is profound; it suggests that the right environment can bring out the latent potential in individuals, aligning personal growth trajectories with organizational success.

This transformative potential extends to how conflict and differences are managed within a team. An effective culture doesn't shy away from conflict but approaches it constructively. Differences in opinion and approach can be the seedbed for innovation if navigated thoughtfully. Companies that master the art of healthy conflict create a culture that harnesses the creative power of diverse viewpoints while maintaining a cohesive team spirit.

Employee empowerment is another cornerstone of a successful culture. When employees feel empowered to take initiative and make decisions, they are more invested in their work and the company's goals. A culture that empowers its people is one that trusts them, and this trust is reciprocated in commitment and a strong work ethic. Empowerment also encourages a sense of ownership, where employees feel responsible for the culture they are a part of and contribute actively to its preservation and evolution.

As the cultural fit puzzle comes together, it forms a picture of an environment where every individual can find their place and thrive. It's about creating a space where differences are not just tolerated but valued, where employees are not just working but growing, and where the company's success is intrinsically tied to the well-being and development of its people.

Moreover, the concept of cultural fit must be dynamic, allowing for shifts and changes as the company grows and the external environment evolves. Stagnation is the antithesis of a healthy culture. A company's culture must be like a living organism, capable of evolution and adaptation, responding to the needs of its employees and the demands of the market.

Ultimately, solving the cultural fit puzzle is about more than just assembling a group of people who can work well together. It's about creating a symphony of talents, where each individual's unique abilities contribute to a harmonious collective output. It's about building a culture where the whole is greater than the sum of its parts, where each person's contributions are recognized and celebrated, and where the culture itself becomes a magnet for talent and a driver of sustainable success.

As the tech industry continues to push the boundaries of what's possible, the cultural fit puzzle remains a central challenge for companies seeking to excel. Those that approach it with a commitment to inclusivity, empowerment, and ongoing growth will find themselves not only assembling productive teams but nurturing an environment where innovation flourishes and where people can do their best work.

To conclude, the cultural fit puzzle within the tech industry is a multifaceted challenge that goes beyond mere technical skill alignment. It's about forging a symbiotic relationship between individuals and the organizational ethos, where soft skills, adaptability, and a shared vision are as critical as proficiency in programming. Cultivating an environment that values these soft elements and recognizes their role in collective achievement is essential for any organization looking to thrive.

Successfully navigating this puzzle requires a delicate balance of maintaining core values while embracing the diversity that fuels innovation and growth. It's about understanding that cultural fit isn't a static metric but a dynamic and evolving quality that needs nurturing. Companies that invest in this understanding are poised to build robust teams that not only share a common purpose but are also equipped to handle the complexities of a rapidly evolving tech landscape.

Ultimately, the cultural fit puzzle isn't about finding candidates who fit the existing mold but about curating a workforce that can grow with the company, contributing to a vibrant, inclusive, and dynamic culture. In resolving this puzzle, companies don't just find the right talent for today—they lay the groundwork for a resilient and innovative organization that is prepared for the challenges of tomorrow. This chapter serves as a guide for organizations striving to understand the intricacies of cultural fit and its profound impact on the success of teams and the broader enterprise.

7

Diversity in Coding: Unlocking Untapped Talent

Diversity in the world of programming is not just a matter of social responsibility or ethical imperative; it is a proven driver of innovation, creativity, and economic growth. Yet, the diversity gap in the tech sector persists, with significant underrepresentation of various groups, including women, people of color, individuals with disabilities, and those from underprivileged socioeconomic backgrounds. This gap is not merely a symptom of a flawed system but a significant contributor to the ongoing talent shortage in the tech industry.

The impact of this diversity gap on the talent pool is profound. When entire segments of the population are underrepresented in the programming field, the industry misses out on a wealth of perspectives and ideas. Diverse teams are more likely to produce innovative solutions because they bring a variety of experiences and viewpoints to the table, challenging each other's assumptions and broadening the collective thinking.

Addressing this issue requires an honest examination of the barriers that contribute to the diversity gap. These can range from biases in hiring practices to a lack of support and mentorship for underrepresented groups within educational and professional settings. Social stereotypes and cultural expectations can also deter individuals from pursuing or continuing a career in tech.

To unlock the potential of a diverse talent pool, the industry must implement successful strategies for inclusion. This begins with education and outreach, creating pathways for underrepresented groups to discover and cultivate an interest in coding from a young age. Schools, universities, and tech companies can partner to provide access to coding classes, workshops, and mentorship programs that demystify the field and empower a wider array of people to consider a career in programming.

Recruitment practices must also evolve. Rather than relying solely on traditional credentials, such as degrees from prestigious institutions, companies are increasingly recognizing the value of non-traditional educational backgrounds, self-taught skills, and life experiences that contribute to a programmer's unique approach to problem-solving.

Inclusion doesn't stop at hiring; it must be woven into the fabric of the company culture. Creating an environment where all employees feel valued and supported is essential. This means offering robust onboarding processes, professional development opportunities, and fostering a workplace where diverse opinions are heard and respected.

Additionally, tapping into diverse perspectives isn't just about bringing different people into the room; it's about giving them a voice. Encouraging participation and leadership from underrepresented groups in meetings, projects, and decision-making processes ensures that diverse perspectives are not only present but active and influential.

Mentorship and sponsorship programs within organizations can play a pivotal role in nurturing talent from diverse backgrounds. By pairing individuals with mentors who can guide and advocate for them, companies can help bridge the gap between diverse talent and leadership opportunities.

It's also important to measure progress and hold organizations accountable. Setting diversity goals and transparently reporting on them can motivate companies to make tangible changes. Regular assessments of diversity metrics and their correlation to business outcomes can reinforce the importance of these initiatives.

By embracing a multiplicity of backgrounds, experiences, and ways of thinking, the programming field can tap into a wellspring of creativity and innovation.

Closing the diversity gap also means tackling subconscious biases that often go unaddressed. From the wording in job postings to the structure of interviews, every stage in the hiring and retention process needs to be scrutinized. Initiatives such as blind recruitment, where identifying details are removed from applications, can help mitigate bias and ensure that talent alone determines who moves forward.

Workplace initiatives that support work-life balance, such as flexible working hours, can also make the tech industry more accessible to those with varying personal responsibilities. Such policies can help retain employees who might otherwise leave the profession due to rigid or demanding work environments.

Additionally, creating employee resource groups and diversity committees can give underrepresented employees a platform to share their experiences and insights, contributing to policy-making and company culture. These groups can help foster a sense of community and belonging, which is crucial for retention and engagement.

Beyond internal policies, companies can make a broader impact by supporting coding education and technology initiatives in underserved communities. By investing in these communities, companies can help cultivate a new generation of programmers and demonstrate a commitment to diversity and inclusion that extends beyond their organizational boundaries.

Equity in professional development and advancement opportunities is also critical. Ensuring that all employees have the same opportunity to grow and advance in their careers can help prevent the funneling of underrepresented groups into lower-level positions without a clear path to leadership.

Networking opportunities, mentorship programs, and clear, merit-based criteria for advancement are important pieces of the puzzle. They help ensure that everyone, regardless of background, has the opportunity to develop professionally and contribute to the industry in meaningful ways.

In fostering a culture that values and seeks out diversity, companies also need to recognize and celebrate the variety of cultures, holidays, and experiences that their employees bring. This acknowledgment can help employees from all backgrounds feel seen and appreciated for their whole selves, not just their professional contributions.

Ultimately, embracing diversity in coding means committing to an ongoing process of learning, unlearning, and relearning. It's about understanding that a diverse workforce is not a box to be checked but a continuous journey towards a more equitable, innovative, and successful industry. Through intentional actions and systemic changes, the tech industry can begin to unlock the full spectrum of untapped talent, benefiting businesses and communities alike.

Broadening the scope of diversity initiatives, companies are increasingly looking to measure the impact of such efforts not only on workforce composition but also on innovation and market reach. By aligning diversity efforts with business outcomes, organizations can create compelling narratives for the value of inclusion. This alignment helps to ensure that diversity and inclusion are not sidelined as ancillary initiatives but are central to the company's strategy and performance.

Engagement with educational institutions is another critical avenue for addressing the diversity gap. By collaborating with schools, universities, and coding bootcamps, companies can influence curricula, provide real-world learning opportunities, and foster a pipeline of diverse talent early on. Scholarship programs, internships, and mentorships directed towards underrepresented groups can make a significant impact on who sees programming as a viable and welcoming career path.

Companies are also reevaluating their cultural symbols and internal communications to ensure they reflect and respect diversity. From the images on the company's website to the language used in internal newsletters, every aspect of communication should send a clear message of inclusivity.

Furthermore, fostering a culture of inclusivity extends to customer and client relationships. Products and services that cater to a diverse user base require input from a diverse group of creators. This inclusive approach to product development not only improves market relevance but also drives innovation by incorporating a wide array of user perspectives.

To facilitate a culture that embraces diversity, leadership training is crucial. Leaders at all levels should be equipped to manage and value diverse teams. This training includes understanding the dynamics of diversity, equity, and inclusion, and the skills to create an environment where all team members can thrive.

By actively seeking to understand and dismantle the systemic barriers that contribute to the diversity gap, the tech industry can cultivate an environment that truly represents the society it serves. It's about creating a space where everyone has the opportunity to participate, contribute, and succeed.

As this exploration of diversity in coding illustrates, unlocking untapped talent requires a multi-faceted and sustained effort. It's about building a culture that not only values diversity in theory but actively pursues it in practice. Through a commitment to inclusion at every level, the tech industry can begin to close the diversity gap and, in doing so, unlock a reservoir of creativity, resilience, and competitive advantage.

Universities), as well as other institutions serving minority groups. These partnerships can create tailored programs that equip students with the in-demand skills they need to succeed in the tech industry while also providing a direct recruitment pipeline for companies.

Another key strategy is the implementation of inclusive hiring practices. This involves re-evaluating job descriptions, recruitment strategies, and interview processes to eliminate biases that may deter or disadvantage diverse candidates. For example, utilizing software that anonymizes applications can help mitigate unconscious biases and ensure a fairer selection process.

In the workplace, affinity groups and employee resource groups (ERGs) offer community support and advocacy for underrepresented employees. These groups can provide a sense of belonging and a safe space for sharing experiences and challenges. They also serve as a resource for the company, offering insights into how to improve the work environment and retain diverse talent.

Leadership development is also a critical area of focus. By identifying and nurturing diverse individuals with leadership potential, companies can build a more inclusive leadership team that reflects the diversity of their workforce and customer base. This, in turn, can inspire others within underrepresented groups to aspire to such roles, knowing that advancement is attainable.

Encouraging a culture of continuous learning and education can further help to address diversity issues. Providing resources for ongoing training and professional development, as well as fostering a culture where employees are encouraged to expand their knowledge and skills, can help break down barriers to advancement.

A critical component of these strategies is the active engagement of senior leadership. When company leaders are visibly committed to diversity and inclusion, it sets a tone for the entire organization. Leadership must be involved in diversity initiatives, not just as sponsors but as active participants, ensuring that these values are integrated into the company's operations and strategic goals.

Lastly, measuring the effectiveness of diversity initiatives is key to understanding their impact. Regularly reviewing workforce diversity metrics and the outcomes of diversity programs helps organizations to assess their progress and identify areas where further work is needed. Transparently sharing these metrics and progress reports can build trust and show a genuine commitment to creating a more diverse and inclusive workplace.

By implementing these strategies, the tech industry can work towards closing the diversity gap and unlocking the full potential of untapped talent. The ultimate goal is to foster an environment where a rich tapestry of backgrounds and perspectives can thrive, driving innovation and reflecting the diversity of the global marketplace the industry serves.

8

Retention: The Art of Keeping a Good Programmer

In the competitive landscape of the tech industry, retention of top talent has become as significant a challenge as recruitment. Companies pour substantial resources into attracting skilled programmers, yet keeping them is an art that many are still learning to master. Understanding why retention can be difficult is essential for companies looking to maintain a strong and innovative workforce.

One of the primary reasons companies struggle with retention is the rapidly evolving nature of technology itself. Programmers often seek environments where they can continuously learn and work on the cutting edge of new technologies. If a company fails to provide opportunities for growth or is slow to adopt new technologies, it risks losing its programmers to organizations that are more technologically progressive.

Workplace culture also plays a pivotal role in retention. Programmers, like all professionals, want to work in environments where they feel respected, valued, and part of a community. A culture that fosters collaboration, creativity, and open communication can significantly enhance job satisfaction. Conversely, a toxic or unsupportive environment can drive even the most dedicated employees to look elsewhere.

Another factor is the alignment of personal values with company values. Programmers often seek out companies whose missions resonate with their own personal beliefs and aspirations. They want to contribute to projects that they feel have a positive impact on society. When there's a misalignment, programmers may feel less engaged with their work, which can prompt them to move on.

Moreover, the issue of work-life balance has come to the forefront. The tech industry is notorious for its demanding work hours, which can lead to burnout and dissatisfaction. Companies that provide a better balance, with flexible working conditions and recognition of personal time, will often have better success in retaining their staff.

Compensation and benefits are, of course, significant factors as well. Programmers know their worth in the market and will naturally gravitate towards opportunities that offer competitive salaries, bonuses, and benefits. However, it's not just about the money. Benefits that improve quality of life, such as health insurance, parental leave, and retirement plans, are also crucial for long-term retention.

Exploring what programmers want from their careers reveals a multi-faceted set of expectations. Beyond competitive compensation, programmers look for opportunities to solve meaningful problems and make a noticeable impact. They value workplaces that support continuous learning and certifications in new skills. They seek recognition for their contributions, not just in terms of promotions or raises, but also through leadership opportunities and the autonomy to lead projects or make significant technical decisions.

Programmers often prefer environments that are less hierarchical and more meritocratic, where ideas are judged on their value rather than the seniority of the person presenting them. They thrive in cultures that are inclusive and diverse, where a variety of perspectives are welcomed and where everyone has the opportunity to succeed.

To retain top programming talent, companies must create an environment that addresses these desires. It's about building a workplace that not only draws talent but nourishes and retains it. This chapter explores the complexities of retention in the tech industry and the strategies companies can implement to keep their best programmers engaged, satisfied, and on board for the long haul.

In the pursuit of retention, personal development plans tailored to each programmer's career goals can be instrumental. Companies that invest time in understanding and supporting the individual aspirations of their programmers tend to have higher retention rates. Such plans could include a clear progression path, opportunities for upskilling, and support for personal projects that align with the company's objectives.

Feedback loops are another retention tool. Regular, constructive feedback helps programmers feel seen and heard, and it assures them that their growth is a priority for the organization. This can include peer reviews, 360-degree feedback mechanisms, and open-door policies that encourage direct communication with management.

Engagement strategies that go beyond the workspace can also reinforce a sense of belonging and loyalty. Team-building retreats, hackathons, innovation labs, and involvement in community tech events can foster a sense of unity and shared purpose.

Workplace flexibility is increasingly important to programmers, who often value autonomy over their work schedule and environment. Companies that offer remote work options, flexible hours, and a results-oriented work environment can be more appealing to top talent looking for a better work-life balance.

Recognition programs that highlight outstanding work and significant contributions can also boost morale and retention. Whether through awards, public acknowledgment, or tangible rewards like bonuses or extra vacation days, recognizing programmers' efforts demonstrates appreciation for their hard work.

Moreover, the introduction of 'stay interviews' can help organizations understand what keeps their employees satisfied and what might cause them to leave. Unlike exit interviews, which are conducted after an employee has already decided to depart, stay interviews proactively engage with staff to uncover and address potential issues before they lead to resignation.

Finally, creating leadership and mentorship roles within the programming team can give experienced programmers a sense of progression without moving into management, which they may not desire. These roles allow them to share their knowledge, shape new hires, and influence the direction of projects, which can be highly satisfying for those who are passionate about the technical side of their careers.

To retain the best programmers, companies must cultivate an environment that not only meets the basic requirements of a good workplace but also goes above and beyond to address the unique needs and aspirations of these highly skilled individuals. This chapter delves into the strategies and practices that can create such an environment, ensuring that the programmers who drive innovation and excellence remain motivated and committed members of the team.

Retention, then, is not just a matter of addressing immediate concerns but requires a forward-looking approach that considers the future trajectory of the programming profession itself. As the role of programmers continues to evolve with technological advancements, companies need to anticipate the kinds of projects and technologies that will excite and engage their technical staff in the long term.

One emerging approach is the creation of internal innovation programs where programmers can pitch and work on new ideas that may be outside of the company's current project scope. These programs can provide a creative outlet and a sense of ownership and can even lead to new product lines or services for the company.

Moreover, companies are beginning to recognize the importance of offering a sense of purpose. Programmers today are not just looking for a job; they're looking for a way to contribute to something larger than themselves. Organizations that connect their work to wider societal impacts often find that their employees are more engaged and committed.

Creating an environment that supports mental health and well-being is also crucial for retention. This includes not only health benefits and wellness programs but also a company culture that recognizes the importance of mental health. Initiatives like no-meeting days, mental health days off, and support for stress management reflect a company's understanding of the pressures associated with tech jobs.

Furthermore, fostering a culture where risk-taking is encouraged and failures are viewed as learning opportunities can lead to greater job satisfaction. Programmers often thrive in environments where they are free to experiment and innovate without fear of negative repercussions for taking calculated risks.

The commitment to retention must be consistent and visible at all levels of the organization. From the C-suite to team leads, all levels of management should demonstrate a commitment to the principles and practices that support retention. This includes actively listening to employees' concerns and suggestions and being willing to make changes based on their feedback.

In conclusion, a company's ability to retain top programming talent hinges on its commitment to creating an environment that not only aligns with the programmers' current needs but also supports their growth, values their well-being, and stimulates their desire to innovate and contribute to the greater good. This holistic approach to retention can turn the challenge of keeping good programmers into an opportunity to build a loyal, innovative, and highly effective technical team.

Navigating the nuances of retention requires recognizing that each programmer is an individual with unique aspirations, motivators, and life circumstances. A one-size-fits-all approach to retention is often ineffective; instead, personalized attention to career paths and individual needs is key.

Programmers may be driven by various factors, including the desire for challenging work, the need for recognition, the pursuit of a healthy work-life balance, or the aspiration to make a meaningful impact on the world. Companies that take the time to understand and address these drivers can create a culture where programmers feel genuinely motivated and invested.

A culture of open communication can further enhance retention. Encouraging programmers to voice their ideas, concerns, and feedback without fear of retribution creates a sense of empowerment and belonging. This communication should be a two-way street, where management also shares its vision, changes, and recognitions transparently with the team.

Providing opportunities for community involvement and social impact can also resonate with programmers who look beyond the technical aspects of their job. Companies that facilitate participation in tech-for-good projects or community outreach can offer fulfilling experiences that align with the values of their employees.

Furthermore, adapting to the changing expectations regarding the workplace is vital. With the rise of remote work and the increasing importance of digital connectivity, companies that offer flexibility in work location and hours can have an edge in retention. However, they must also work to maintain a sense of team cohesion and shared culture, even when the physical office is no longer the daily point of connection.

Lastly, retention is about looking ahead, preparing not just for the future of technology, but for the future of work itself. This means staying ahead of industry trends, forecasting the skills that will be in demand, and ensuring that employees are well-positioned to meet those future needs. It's about creating an environment that not only responds to the present but anticipates and shapes the future.

A strategic approach to retention, grounded in an understanding of what programmers value and what drives them, can transform the challenge of keeping good programmers into a defining strength of a tech company. It requires commitment, flexibility, and a willingness to invest in people as the ultimate innovators and drivers of success.

Retention strategies that embrace the evolving landscape of work-life integration are gaining traction. Today's programmers often seek flexibility not just in schedule but also in how they approach their work. Employing a variety of work models, from fully remote to hybrid options, allows individuals to tailor their work environment to their personal productivity styles, which can lead to greater job satisfaction and retention.

Additionally, investing in the right tools and technology that facilitate remote collaboration is critical. Providing a seamless virtual workspace ensures that all team members, regardless of location, have equal access to participate and contribute meaningfully to projects.

Another key aspect of retention is the provision of competitive and equitable compensation packages that reflect the value programmers bring to the organization. This goes beyond just salary; it includes equity offerings, bonuses, and other financial incentives that align employees' success with that of the company.

Companies are also realizing the importance of mental health and wellness programs. From offering subscriptions to meditation apps to providing in-house counseling services, these programs show a commitment to the holistic well-being of employees. When programmers feel cared for on a personal level, their loyalty to the company strengthens.

A proactive approach to career development is equally critical. Providing clear pathways for advancement, ongoing education, and skill development encourages employees to envision a long-term future with the company. This could include offering stipends for continuing education, sponsoring conference attendance, or providing in-house workshops and training sessions.

For retention to be truly effective, it must also be inclusive. Cultivating a workplace where diversity is celebrated and all employees feel they can be themselves without fear of discrimination is vital. This involves regular training on unconscious bias, diversity, and inclusion, and fostering a workplace where diversity in all its forms is genuinely valued and leveraged for the collective benefit.

In a fast-paced industry, ensuring that employees feel connected to the larger vision and direction of the company is also important. When programmers see their work contributing to significant achievements and innovations, they are more likely to feel engaged and motivated to stay.

Continuous improvement in retention strategies is essential, as what works today may not be as effective tomorrow. Soliciting regular feedback from employees, staying abreast of industry best practices, and being willing to adapt and iterate on strategies are all part of creating a dynamic and responsive retention policy.

In essence, retention is an ongoing commitment to creating an environment where programmers can excel, feel valued, and see a future for themselves. By focusing on the factors that drive satisfaction and loyalty, companies can not only retain their best talent but also create a culture of excellence that attracts even more top-tier programmers.

The art of retention is an ongoing commitment to understanding and fulfilling the needs and aspirations of programmers. It's about creating a culture that not only values their technical skills but also respects their individuality, nurtures their growth, and recognizes their contributions. A successful retention strategy is comprehensive, addressing everything from competitive compensation to professional development, from work-life balance to a culture of inclusivity and respect.

Programmers are the lifeblood of any tech company, and their retention is critical to sustaining innovation and competitive edge. Companies that excel in retention recognize that their employees are their most valuable asset and that the health of their workforce directly impacts the health of their business. By cultivating an environment that programmers are reluctant to leave, these companies ensure that their teams remain robust and dynamic.

Retention, therefore, is not just about preventing turnover; it's about fostering an environment where employees are so engaged and satisfied that leaving doesn't cross their minds. It's a holistic approach, weaving together the various threads that influence a programmer's workplace experience into a cohesive tapestry that supports their career journey.

As the tech industry continues to evolve at a rapid pace, the strategies for retention will also need to adapt. Companies that remain attuned to the changing needs of their workforce and are proactive in their retention efforts will not only keep their best programmers but will also attract new talent looking for an employer that values their contributions and well-being.

As we forge ahead in an industry that never stands still, the conversation on retention must also progress. It's critical for companies to stay engaged with their employees, continually reassessing the effectiveness of retention strategies and staying open to new ideas.

For example, as new technologies emerge and the nature of programming work evolves, what motivates and retains programmers may shift. Companies must be ready to evolve their offerings, whether that means embracing new work models, enhancing their technological toolsets, or providing opportunities for their employees to engage with cutting-edge projects.

Looking to the future, the role of AI and machine learning in shaping the workplace will also influence retention strategies. Tools that help understand employee satisfaction and predict turnover risks can enable proactive retention efforts. However, the human element will always remain central; technology should aid, not replace, the genuine human connections and understanding that underpin a great workplace culture.

Moreover, the rising trend of gig work and the freelance economy has implications for how companies think about retention. Offering flexible project-based work or engaging with employees as internal 'entre-preneurs' can provide the balance between independence and belonging that many seek.

In the broader scope, retention is about building a community within the workplace—a place where individuals don't just come to work, but come to grow, to be challenged, and to contribute to something they believe in. It's about ensuring that every programmer feels like an integral part of the company's journey and success.

In conclusion, retention is much more than a human resources objec-tive; it's a fundamental business strategy that requires insight, agility, and a genuine commitment to the individuals behind the code. As companies master the art of keeping good programmers, they not only create a stable foundation for their operations but also cultivate an environment where innovation thrives and the full potential of every employee can be realized.

9

The Global Search for Programming Excellence

Globalization has significantly expanded the horizons of the tech industry's hunt for programming talent. No longer confined by geographical boundaries, companies can tap into a global pool of expertise, looking for the best and brightest, irrespective of their location. This shift has not only broadened access to talent but also intensified competition among companies to attract and retain skilled programmers.

The globalization of the talent search has been facilitated by advances in communication technology, which have made remote collaboration more feasible than ever before. Teams spread across different continents can work together as seamlessly as if they were in the same room, thanks to high-speed internet, collaborative software, and cloud technologies.

This global perspective has important implications for the way companies approach the recruitment and management of talent. It opens the door to diversity of thought and experience, as programmers from different cultural and educational backgrounds bring unique perspectives to problem-solving and innovation. However, it also presents challenges in terms of coordinating across time zones, managing diverse teams, and creating a cohesive company culture.

Remote work, in particular, has become a key factor in the global search for programming excellence. The rise of remote work arrangements has allowed companies to overcome local talent shortages and reduce costs associated with maintaining physical office spaces. For programmers, remote work offers the flexibility to live anywhere, eliminating long commutes and providing the opportunity to balance work with personal life more effectively.

International talent plays a crucial role in filling the talent void in regions where skilled programmers are in short supply. By recruiting internationally, companies not only address immediate staffing needs but also enrich their teams with global insights and experiences. This can be a particular advantage when developing products and services for a global market.

However, leveraging international talent requires companies to navigate a complex web of visa regulations, employment laws, and cultural considerations. Successful global recruitment strategies are underpinned by a solid understanding of these factors and a commitment to supporting international hires through relocation, integration, and ongoing support.

The implications for programming talent are significant. Programmers now have more opportunities than ever to work for leading companies without the need to relocate. They can compete on a global stage, showcasing their skills to a wide array of potential employers. For some, this means greater job security and the opportunity to work on more diverse projects; for others, it presents the chance to work for companies they admire without leaving their home country or community.

The global search for programming excellence underscores the importance of a strategic approach to talent management that recognizes the boundless nature of the tech industry today. In this chapter, we explore how companies can effectively navigate the global talent marketplace and how remote work and international hiring can be optimized to create dynamic, diverse, and successful programming teams.

As the search for programming talent becomes increasingly global, companies are adapting their talent acquisition strategies to be more inclusive and wide-reaching. They are utilizing online platforms, social media, and international recruiting agencies to connect with potential hires in every corner of the world. By doing so, they tap into a wealth of talent that was previously inaccessible, opening up a realm of possibilities for innovation and growth.

The use of talent analytics has also become crucial in the global talent hunt. By analyzing data on talent pools, employment trends, and skill sets, companies can make more informed decisions on where to focus their recruiting efforts. This data-driven approach allows them to identify talent hotspots around the globe and target their recruitment strategies accordingly.

Remote work has not only expanded the talent pool but has also necessitated a shift in the way companies onboard and integrate new hires. Remote onboarding processes that are thoughtful and comprehensive can set the stage for long-term success, even when face-to-face interaction is limited. This includes virtual meet-and-greets, online training modules, and digital toolkits that help remote employees feel connected and engaged from day one.

The management of global, remote teams requires a different set of skills and tools. Managers must be adept at leading across cultures, facilitating virtual communication, and building trust without the benefit of physical presence. They must also be sensitive to the various challenges remote work can present, such as isolation or the blurring of work-life boundaries, and be prepared to address these issues proactively.

In addition to logistical considerations, companies must also grapple with the legal and regulatory challenges of employing international talent. This includes understanding the intricacies of work visas, tax laws, and labor regulations that vary from country to country. A strong legal framework and compliance infrastructure are essential to navigate these complexities effectively.

The role of international talent in filling the talent void is multi-faceted. On one hand, it's about addressing the practical needs of the industry. On the other, it's about fostering a more diverse and inclusive workforce that can drive creativity and innovation. Diverse teams that bring together a range of cultural backgrounds and experiences are more likely to challenge conventional thinking and develop unique solutions to complex problems.

For programmers, the global marketplace offers unprecedented opportunities for career development. It enables them to work on international projects, collaborate with diverse teams, and gain exposure to different approaches and methodologies. It also encourages a more flexible and autonomous working style, which can lead to greater job satisfaction and work-life balance.

As we move forward, the global search for programming excellence is set to redefine the tech industry. It challenges companies to think bigger and broader when it comes to talent acquisition and management. It also empowers programmers to seek out the best opportunities for their skills, regardless of their geographic location. This chapter explores the nuances of this global movement and its profound implications for both employers and employees in the tech industry.

Embracing this global movement, companies are increasingly recognizing the need for cultural competence in their teams. Cultural training programs are being implemented to help employees understand and navigate the complexities of working with a globally diverse team. These programs aim to foster an inclusive environment where every team member feels valued and understood, regardless of cultural background.

The global talent landscape also brings into focus the need for flexible and diverse work arrangements. Companies are adopting a variety of work models, from fully remote teams to hybrid models and co-working spaces that cater to international employees. This flexibility is not only a response to the varying preferences and needs of a global workforce but also a strategic move to ensure business continuity in a world where local events can disrupt work.

For programmers, the global talent market means that continuous learning and skill development are more critical than ever. With the competition no longer limited by geography, staying ahead requires a commitment to lifelong learning and the ability to adapt to new tools, languages, and development methodologies.

The potential of remote work and international talent to fill the void left by local talent shortages has prompted some regions to offer incentives to attract tech companies and remote workers. This includes tax breaks, grants, and infrastructure support aimed at creating tech hubs and fostering innovation ecosystems.

However, the shift towards a global search for talent is not without its challenges. Language barriers, time zone differences, and collaboration across distances can create hurdles in project management and team dynamics. Companies are investing in technology and training to mitigate these challenges, including the use of synchronous and asynchronous communication tools, flexible scheduling, and project management software that can accommodate the needs of a dispersed team.

The integration of international talent also raises important questions about equity and fairness. Ensuring that remote employees have equal access to opportunities, recognition, and career advancement is vital for maintaining morale and retaining global talent. Companies are developing metrics and monitoring systems to ensure that all employees, regardless of location, are evaluated based on their contributions and performance.

The global search for programming excellence is transforming the tech industry into a more dynamic, interconnected, and innovative space. It provides an exciting opportunity for companies to leverage a vast pool of talent and for programmers to expand their horizons. As companies and individuals navigate this global landscape, the values of diversity, inclusion, flexibility, and continuous improvement stand as pillars for future success in the digital age.

The global search for excellence in programming has initiated a transformation not just in hiring practices, but also in the way work itself is conceptualized and organized. As remote work dissolves geographic boundaries, it cultivates a new kind of workplace—one that is omnipresent and dynamic, allowing for a 24-hour work cycle where different time zones can become an advantage rather than a challenge.

This round-the-clock productivity can lead to an acceleration in project timelines and potentially continuous support for users in different regions. It can also allow for a more responsive and agile development process, as teams across the globe can pass tasks from one time zone to the next, effectively creating a 'follow-the-sun' workflow.

However, this non-stop cycle also prompts a reassessment of work-life balance and the health of programmers, who may find themselves needing to interact with colleagues and clients across disparate time zones. Companies are therefore tasked with creating policies that protect their employees' personal time while still allowing for the flexibility required by international collaboration.

To facilitate this global collaboration, companies are also investing in advanced project management tools and platforms that enhance transparency and coordination. Cloud-based tools and platforms that support real-time editing, version control, and task management are becoming integral to maintaining cohesion across distributed teams.

Moreover, the dispersion of the workforce is leading to new forms of team building and corporate culture. Virtual team-building activities, online social events, and digital 'water coolers' are becoming commonplace, helping to maintain a sense of camaraderie and team unity.

In this rapidly expanding global marketplace, the demand for multilingual and culturally fluent programmers is on the rise. Language skills are becoming as valuable as programming languages, and cultural fluency is increasingly seen as a key competency for professionals who can navigate and bridge the nuances of a multicultural team.

As the industry moves forward, it is clear that the future of programming will be deeply influenced by this global talent search. The companies and individuals who thrive will be those who can embrace diversity, flexibility, and the boundless opportunities presented by this global paradigm.

The journey towards programming excellence, therefore, transcends borders and unites diverse talents in pursuit of shared goals. It's a journey that promises not just more robust technological solutions, but also a more inclusive and innovative future for the tech industry at large. This chapter not only maps out the terrain of this global search but also serves as a guide for navigating the rich and complex tapestry of the world's programming talent.

Companies that cast a wide net and engage in a global search for talent open themselves up to a wealth of benefits. By not limiting their hiring to a local talent pool, organizations can access a broader array of skill sets, experiences, and cultural perspectives. This approach aligns well with the tech industry's inherent global reach and the collaborative nature of coding, where projects often span different countries and continents.

A global search is more than just an answer to local talent shortages; it's a strategic move that can bring fresh ideas and innovative problem-solving approaches. However, it comes with its own set of challenges, such as navigating different time zones, languages, and cultural nuances. Companies must be prepared to invest in the tools and communication strategies that can bridge these gaps, fostering a cohesive and inclusive work environment for all employees, regardless of their location.

Moreover, a global talent search emphasizes the need for strong remote work infrastructures. As companies attract and hire talent from around the world, they must also adapt their workflows and management styles to support a distributed workforce. This includes establishing clear communication channels, creating opportunities for remote team bonding, and developing remote-friendly company policies.

Continuing with the topic of a global search for programming talent, it's important to emphasize the significance of establishing a strong support system for international hires. Integrating employees from around the world involves more than accommodating different time zones; it's about fostering a culture that respects and embraces diversity in all its forms.

Companies that excel in global recruitment often implement

comprehensive relocation assistance programs to ease the transition for employees moving to a new country. These programs can include language training, assistance with visas and legal requirements, and help with finding housing and schools. For remote employees, virtual assistance to set up a home office and understand local tax implications can be equally valuable.

To make a global team work effectively, companies also invest in collaboration technology that transcends geographical barriers. This includes robust project management software, real-time communication tools, and platforms that facilitate asynchronous work. Creating a digital workspace where team members can collaborate as if they were in the same room is crucial for the cohesion of a distributed team.

In addition, fostering an inclusive workplace where all employees—regardless of their location—feel valued and heard is critical. This might involve rotating meeting times to accommodate different time zones, celebrating international holidays, or hosting virtual events that bring the team together.

Companies also need to be aware of cultural differences and the impact these can have on work styles and communication. Cultural competency training can help team members understand and appreciate each other's backgrounds and work effectively across cultures.

Global talent search strategies should also be compliant with international labor laws and practices. This requires a nuanced understanding of the legal and regulatory frameworks governing employment in different countries. Partnering with local experts and legal advisors can help ensure that the company's hiring practices are respectful and equitable across all regions.

Finally, the global search for talent should be seen as a continuous process, not a one-time initiative. Building a pipeline of global talent involves long-term relationships with international recruiting agencies, participation in global tech conferences, and active engagement with worldwide tech communities.

By adopting a strategic and culturally sensitive approach to global recruitment, companies can not only enrich their talent pool but also enhance their global competitiveness. The global search for programming talent is an opportunity to push the boundaries of innovation, drive growth, and reflect the global audience that technology serves.

The pursuit of a global search for programmers also demonstrates a company's commitment to diversity and inclusion. It signals an understanding that talent exists everywhere and that the best teams are often those that reflect a range of backgrounds and experiences.

10

Technology Trends and Future Skills

In an industry characterized by rapid evolution, the only constant is change. Technology trends are not merely passing fads; they are the harbingers of the new realities that shape our digital world. Anticipating the impact of emerging technologies on the demand for programmer expertise is crucial for staying relevant. As we stand on the cusp of innovations like quantum computing, advanced artificial intelligence, blockchain revolutions, and beyond, the skill set required of programmers continues to evolve.

The increasing integration of AI and machine learning in various sectors is revolutionizing how we approach problem-solving and product development. Programmers must not only understand the foundations of these technologies but also how to apply them creatively to industry-specific challenges. Similarly, the expansion of the Internet of Things (IoT) ecosystem demands programmers who can navigate the complexities of connected devices and the data they generate.

Emerging technologies also bring new responsibilities. Ethical considerations, particularly in AI development, require a programmer's expertise to extend beyond the technical to the philosophical and moral implications of their work. Understanding the potential societal impact of technology will become increasingly important.

Preparing the next generation of programmers for these waves of technological advancement involves a multifaceted approach. Education systems must adapt, emphasizing not just coding skills but also critical thinking, creativity, and an understanding of cross-disciplinary applications. Curriculums must be agile, incorporating current industry trends and tools so that students graduate with knowledge that is immediately applicable.

Continuous learning is the bedrock of a programmer's career. As such, professional development cannot end with formal education. The industry must support ongoing learning through workshops, seminars, webinars, and conferences that keep programmers up to date with the latest advancements. Companies can play a significant role here by fostering a culture of learning and providing resources for continued education.

Mentorship programs also become increasingly valuable, connecting seasoned experts with new programmers. These relationships can help newer talent navigate the rapidly changing tech landscape and apply emerging technologies effectively in their work.

Cross-disciplinary skill development is another critical area. Programmers who understand the fundamentals of business, healthcare, environmental science, and other fields will be better equipped to apply technological solutions to a broad spectrum of global challenges.

Moreover, the proliferation of open-source platforms has democratized access to cutting-edge tools, allowing programmers from around the world to contribute to and learn from the forefront of technology. Engaging with these communities can provide real-world experience and a forum for collaboration and innovation.

As the digital landscape evolves at a breakneck pace, the foresight into technology trends becomes imperative for shaping the future of programming. Emerging technologies redefine the boundaries of what's possible, and with each advancement, the demand for specific programmer expertise shifts. Anticipating these shifts is crucial for businesses to stay competitive and for educators to prepare the next wave of programmers.

Emerging technologies like artificial intelligence (AI), machine learning, Internet of Things (IoT), blockchain, and quantum computing are not just buzzwords; they are reshaping industries. As these technologies mature, the skill set required for programmers evolves. Proficiency in data science, for instance, has become highly sought after with the rise of big data analytics. Similarly, understanding cybersecurity has moved from a niche skill to a necessary area of expertise for many developers.

To anticipate the impact of such technologies, companies and educational institutions must monitor the technological landscape proactively. Businesses can engage in trend analysis and predictive modeling to understand how innovations might affect their operations and demand for talent. For educational institutions, it means staying connected with industry developments and updating curricula to reflect the skills that will be in demand.

Preparing the next generation of programmers requires a multi-faceted approach. Education must not only teach the technical skills needed to manipulate and create within new technological paradigms but also foster adaptability, critical thinking, and continuous learning. In an environment where the only constant is change, the ability to learn and adapt is as important as any specific technical skill.

Hands-on experience with emerging technologies through internships, apprenticeships, and project-based learning can provide invaluable context for theoretical knowledge. Partnering with tech companies to offer students real-world challenges can bridge the gap between education and industry, ensuring that learning aligns with practical needs.

Moreover, cultivating a mindset geared towards innovation and experimentation is essential. Programmers must be encouraged to explore and innovate beyond the confines of current technologies, envisioning new applications and solutions. Such a mindset will enable them to ride the waves of future tech trends rather than being overtaken by them.

Inclusion in tech education also plays a critical role. By ensuring that underrepresented groups have access to education in emerging tech fields, the industry can benefit from a wider range of perspectives and solutions.

Diversity in thought leads to innovation, and innovation is the currency of the future tech landscape.

The dialogue between industry and academia is critical in preparing programmers for the future. Curriculums need to be agile, updated regularly to reflect the rapid changes in technology. For instance, as cloud computing becomes ubiquitous, understanding distributed systems and cloud infrastructure becomes just as fundamental as traditional computing knowledge.

Mentorship from seasoned professionals can guide new programmers through the nuances of technological application and innovation. Such guidance helps not only in imparting hard skills but also in navigating the tech industry's landscape, understanding its trends, and foreseeing its turning points.

In addition, fostering a culture of continuous professional development within the workplace can ensure that current programmers remain at the forefront of technological advancements. Investment in training and development programs, attending conferences, workshops, and webinars, and even allocating time for personal research and experimentation can all contribute to a workforce that is well-prepared for future demands.

Cross-disciplinary skills are becoming increasingly valuable as technology integrates more deeply into all aspects of life. Programmers with a strong grasp of fields such as biotechnology, environmental science, or digital arts bring a unique perspective to their work. They can see connections and opportunities that others might miss and can contribute to innovative solutions that cross traditional boundaries.

The importance of soft skills continues to grow alongside technical abilities. Collaboration, communication, and problem-solving are essential in a world where teams are often distributed globally and projects can span multiple disciplines and cultures. Programmers who can effectively work in diverse teams and communicate complex ideas clearly will be invaluable in the tech waves of the future.

The key to preparing for the future is flexibility. The tech industry's direction can shift with the emergence of a single new technology, and the ability to pivot and embrace these shifts is essential. Programmers who are versatile and open to change, who can learn new languages and frameworks quickly, and who can apply their skills in a variety of contexts will be the ones who thrive.

As we continue to consider the preparation required for future technological waves, it's clear that versatility will be a defining trait of successful programmers. The programmers who will excel are those who can not only adapt to new languages and frameworks but also anticipate and even drive changes in the industry. They will be the pioneers at the forefront of tech evolution, comfortable with experimenting and pushing boundaries.

The concept of T-shaped skills becomes particularly relevant in this context. Programmers are encouraged to develop deep expertise in at least one area while maintaining a broad knowledge base across multiple facets of technology. This allows them to contribute specialized knowledge and also collaborate across various domains, increasing their value and adaptability in a dynamic market.

The incorporation of emerging technologies into mainstream education is essential. Concepts like AI, blockchain, and quantum computing should be demystified and integrated into learning paths early on, giving new generations a head start in understanding and shaping these fields.

Programming ethics and sustainable development should also be integrated into education and practice. As technology becomes more powerful, its potential to impact society for better or worse grows. Ethical programming and the ability to create technology responsibly will be crucial skills for programmers who will shape the future.

Further, the international community of programmers must be leveraged. Online platforms and forums allow for the sharing of knowledge and challenges across borders, nurturing a global perspective. Exposure to diverse approaches and challenges ensures a more robust problem-solving skill set and a wider vision of the tech landscape.

Active industry-academic partnerships can result in a curriculum that is reflective of real-world demands and provides students with the hands-on experience necessary for true understanding. Internships, co-op programs, and project-based learning initiatives can bridge the gap between theoretical knowledge and practical application.

In this rapidly changing world, lifelong learning becomes not just a benefit but a necessity. The most successful programmers will be those who continually seek to learn, staying curious and engaged with the latest developments. This mindset should be encouraged and supported at all levels, from the individual to the corporate.

To excel in the future, programmers must be as adept at learning new technologies as they are at applying them. They must be visionary in their approach, ethical in their practice, and collaborative in their work ethic. With these attributes, the next generation of programmers will not just ride the waves of technological advancement—they will create them.

The significance of soft skills in the context of future skills cannot be understated. As projects grow increasingly complex and interdisciplinary, the ability of programmers to navigate complex team dynamics, articulate ideas clearly, and integrate feedback constructively will be just as vital as their technical prowess. The programmers of the future will need to be adept communicators, capable of bridging the gap between the technical and non-technical worlds.

A commitment to innovation must also be at the heart of a programmer's career development. The tech industry is driven by innovation, and programmers must be prepared to contribute original ideas and solutions. This requires creative thinking and a thorough understanding of the latest research and development within the tech field. Companies and educational institutions should encourage this innovative mindset, creating spaces for experimentation and exploration.

As we look ahead, the role of artificial intelligence and automation in shaping the future of programming becomes increasingly evident. The programmers of tomorrow will need to understand how to work alongside AI, utilizing these tools to augment their capabilities rather than compete with them. Learning how to design, manage, and collaborate with intelligent systems will be an indispensable skill.

Environmental sustainability is another aspect that future programmers must consider. As global attention shifts towards combating climate change, programmers will need to develop skills in creating efficient and sustainable technologies. This could range from optimizing code to reduce energy consumption to developing software for renewable energy systems.

The global search for programming excellence also implies a need for cultural intelligence. As teams become more global, understanding and respecting cultural differences will be crucial for successful collaboration. Programmers must be equipped to work within diverse teams, respecting different viewpoints and leveraging these differences to create superior solutions.

Lastly, the mental resilience to cope with the fast-paced nature of the tech industry is essential. Programs that support mental health, stress management, and resilience training will be integral in preparing programmers for the high demands of their roles.

In summary, future skills in programming will extend beyond technical knowledge to include soft skills, innovation, AI collaboration, sustainability, cultural intelligence, and mental resilience. Education systems, corporations, and individuals must all play a role in developing these competencies to navigate the exciting and challenging waves of future technology.

11

Conclusion: Crafting the Codebreakers

The exploration into the scarcity of good programmers has spanned the spectrum from education to industry practices, from hiring paradigms to cultural fit, and from diversity to retention strategies. The journey has illuminated the complex web of factors that contribute to the ongoing challenge of finding and nurturing programming talent. Good programmers are, indeed, rare gems—multifaceted and invaluable.

The crux of the scarcity lies not only in the rapidly evolving nature of technology but also in the lagging adaptation of educational systems and workplace environments. While technology leaps forward, educational institutions often struggle to keep pace, and companies sometimes cling to outdated practices that fail to inspire or retain the best minds.

However, the future is bright for those who are prepared to embrace change. We stand on the cusp of a new era in programming—an era marked by a global talent pool, by cultures that value diversity and flexibility, and by technologies that expand the very definition of what it means to be a programmer. The evolution of programming talent will be characterized by an ability to adapt, to learn continuously, and to solve problems with creativity and ethical consideration.

The 'codebreakers' of tomorrow are being crafted today through initiatives that broaden access to education, that reimagine the recruitment process, and that foster work environments where every programmer can thrive. These are the environments where passion for technology is matched by compassion for colleagues, where the pursuit of excellence is a collective endeavor, and where the innovation and leadership of every programmer are recognized and celebrated.

As we look ahead, the evolution of programming talent will undoubtedly be influenced by artificial intelligence, quantum computing, and technologies that we have yet to imagine. Programmers will need to be as adept in their soft skills as they are in their technical skills, able to navigate the complexities of a global workforce and the intricacies of machines that learn and think.

The challenge for both industry and academia will be to continue adapting, to remain vigilant in the face of technological shifts, and to always prioritize the growth and development of their programmers. Crafting the codebreakers of the future is a monumental task, but it is essential for the continued prosperity and progress of our society in the digital age.

As we gaze into the future of programming, it's clear that the role of the programmer is undergoing a profound transformation. The codebreakers of tomorrow will navigate a landscape where programming is not just about writing code but about leveraging technology to solve complex, global challenges. The convergence of fields—where technology meets healthcare, finance, education, and more—will necessitate a breed of programmer who is both a specialist and a generalist, capable of thinking at the intersection of disciplines.

This holistic approach to programming talent development must be mirrored in how we educate, recruit, hire, and nurture this vital workforce. Initiatives that once seemed revolutionary, such as coding bootcamps and hackathons, will become mainstream, serving as both training grounds and proving grounds for talent. Meanwhile, traditional degrees may evolve to become more modular and customizable to keep pace with the rapid innovation in technology.

The shift toward remote and distributed workforces will continue to democratize access to tech jobs, allowing companies to tap into talent from every corner of the globe. This will enrich the tech ecosystem with a diversity of thought that is as vast as the digital realm itself. Yet, it will also require a rethinking of team dynamics and collaboration, as the traditional office becomes a digital workspace without borders.

Ethical considerations will take center stage as the impact of technology on society becomes more evident. Programmers will need to be ethical guardians, ensuring that the digital solutions they create are secure, respectful of privacy, and beneficial to society. The codebreakers will need to be adept not only at constructing digital worlds but also at considering their implications.

In this future, the scarcity of good programmers will be addressed not by lowering standards but by elevating the entire field. We will see a greater emphasis on nurturing talent from a young age and on creating lifelong learning pathways that allow for career shifts and growth. Companies that invest in their people, recognizing the human behind the programmer, will become the most sought-after places to work.

In conclusion, the journey toward "Crafting the Codebreakers" is one of ambition and necessity. As we harness the collective intelligence, creativity, and ethics of the global programming community, we unlock the door to a future that is bright with possibility. The task ahead is to build the frameworks, forge the pathways, and light the beacons that will guide the codebreakers on their journey to excellence. The future is not just what happens next—it's what we choose to make of it. Now is the time to craft the codebreakers who will define tomorrow.